THROUGH THE WARDROBE

Through the Wardrobe

An Exploration of the Embodied Experience of Live-Action Roleplaying

REBECCA MILTON

Melodious Tear

CONTENTS

DEDICATION
vii

~ I ~
The Threads of Our Wakings
1

~ II ~
Voice and Heart
25

~ III ~
Shield on Arm
58

References
80

ACKNOWLEDGEMENTS & NOTES
82
ABOUT THE AUTHOR
85

Copyright © 2020 by Rebecca Milton

All rights reserved. No part of this book may be reproduced in any manner whatsoever without written permission except in the case of brief quotations embodied in critical articles and reviews.

First Printing, 2022

For Jack, Marius,
and all of the others
we'll never get to meet.

~ I ~

THE THREADS OF OUR WAKINGS

There are too many of us in this building. We are crammed together, pressed so close that it feels like we are no longer hundreds of people, but one body of mourning. There are benches ahead, filled with Jack's family, his co-workers, our friends who bore his coffin on their shoulders. People are even stood around the benches, in the aisles - then, there is us. We are the ones who only just made it into the building; more stand out in the cold. We are in the corridor, the cold November wind on the backs of our necks, necks that strain as we look up at the screen that shows us Jack's face.

It was a Wednesday when we found out he had died; Tuesday that he had gone, in that abrupt and sped-up way that young people tend to die. They call it an unexplained cardiac event. I think the world was too small to contain him. You hear people say things like *they were larger than life* - and I'd never understood that until I met Jack.

I spent a week away with him and some other friends, the first year that I met him. A few days into that larp, I had a panic attack so bad that I could barely walk afterwards. Jack carried me the twenty minute walk back to the house where we were staying, somehow managing to make me laugh all the way.

Even at his funeral, I am not alone. I am in my partner's arms, surrounded by friends who I have come to love in the way Jack loved everyone. Eternally, and enduringly, and completely, no matter what happens. Ahead of us are the two friends we visited the day after Jack died, the people who we walked with under a pink and orange streaked sky, telling stories about the silliest things Jack ever did. About the best things. About the things we'll never forget.

They, and a huge number of the hundreds of people here, are my family. My brothers and sisters. At times they have been my lovers and my enemies, my children and my parents, my Gods and my Demons. Our family is one forged through years of fighting wars, and exploring tombs; through breaking into vaults and searching for lost loved ones; through defeating monsters, and being the monsters that are defeated. They are the family who fill the gaps in our heart that we didn't even know were there.

This will not make sense to most people, but then, that is why I am writing this. So that you can understand.

Through the gaps that lie between the heads of my family, I can just about see the lectern. The service leader stands there and introduces Jack's father, who can barely form sentences. His sister, who speaks with such joy and love of the brother she never thought she'd have to worry about losing this soon. Then Carlo takes the stage - Carlo, who is just as bright and brilliant and shining as Jack was, the only person from our family that could possibly have stood for all of us in his honour. He reads a speech that I know he agonised over, because I helped him craft every word. The pain stabs hot into my chest. It didn't hurt this much on the page.

This is the second funeral I have ever been to; I'm hardly an expert on funerals. But I know that they tend to make you think of the person. That's what they're meant to do.

I curl into my sobs and think about the time Jack was dying of the plague, and I offered to kill him.

That will not make sense either.

Let me tell it a different way.

My sparkface is Cateline. I am the Last Storyteller, Mother of the Masks of the Pilgrimhearth, one of the Pilgrims of the Red Coats, and many other things. This story I will tell in the words of all stories, because it is a story of my hearthfire, of a brother who was not a brother, of clouds of pink and gold swirling around me. I am Oracle, one and many, and I am here to give you the story of my Sparkshield.

Marius and I are bound in swords, but not blood. We put eyes on each other many moons ago, when he tried to put my brother Thomas to sleep, just because Marius was bubbling. Thomas did bubble; I did not. I took the Laertes' tools that Marius had used, shrouding some in my womb and casting the rest to Sycorax. I had a cloud to turn it to my Robin's tools and send Marius to the Styx, but later used it as Juliet's hand. This is…not how most put their hands in another's. But this is the story of Marius and I.

I put my hand in his the first time I tried to put him to sleep.

You see, Marius is bathed in the light of the Bright Lady, and Her touch fills him with redness. You can form that cloud into a picture for yourself. In some stories he can bury the redness, march at the side of the other Pilgrims as a shield, but sometimes he becomes a fountain of copper. The redness gets out, and all he can think of is dancing. But it is bright. I am at his side.

The first time that Marius spilled redness over the Pilgrims, I closed my eyes and remembered the time I was King of Scotland, and drew my tools. I crept into his shadow, whilst his eyes lay on the voices of the Pilgrims, and I put my eyes on the spot that would put him to sleep if I remembered my time as a Thane well enough. I let forth a spark that it would not, in fact, put Marius to sleep.

It didn't, not that time, and not in any of the other stories where I had to tell it. Once, we danced a duet, and I had to take the tools of a sleeping coat and read the story of Marius's dancing. It filled me with so much treacle that I might as well have taken off my eyes. But I did dance better than him, and even he would put words to that.

I made sure that I was his own Sparkshield as much as he was mine. That I was in his shadow in every story where he turned red. I carry something too big for me as well, and he has always been there when my voice has sprung forth. It is not a weight he made, just as my voice is not a weight I made. Each day, we carry them, because that is all you can do.

Ah. You won't have understood a word of that, will you. I'm sorry - Cateline doesn't speak normally. She is, in essence, the reincarnated form of the being from whom all prophecy originated - a creature called a 'First', named Oracle. She and her kind were, as you might imagine from the name, the first beings to walk the world. When Oracle died, her Voice - that power of Prophecy - passed to the nearest person, and so on, until it reached Cateline. Cateline not only has that power, but she also has the ability to remember all of those previous lives that the Voice of Oracle travelled through.

This is why Cateline speaks only in metaphor. Her metaphors are a mixture of Shakespearean references, common idioms, synonyms, and references to the adventures she's had with her friends. Sycorax, for example, means 'earth' - a reference to Shakespeare's *Tempest*. Two of the other four elements - Arial (air) and Prospero (water) also take their names from that play. Meanwhile, a 'Red Coat' is someone who is British, and may be specifically a soldier or just generally someone from that country.

You may think that this is wildly complicated, and it is. It may be even more disconcerting to learn that to play Cateline, I literally spoke in this metaphorical language. Often for three days on end; twice for six days. When I would emerge from playing her it would be in a fog, where sometimes I still slipped up and said 'west' instead of 'left' or 'clouds' instead of 'thoughts'. To become her was to reach for every part of myself that loved language and poetry and hold it out to the world. It just...took a while for people to understand.

However, you and I do not have five years for me to show you how Cateline's language developed and what every word means. So let me, instead, ask her to translate.

My name is Cateline. I am the Last Storyteller, a Master of the London Lodge of Freemasons, a member of the Wasteland Commission, and many other things. This is not how I speak, but for the sake of being able to tell you what I mean, I will use your words, even though it hurts me to do so. You see, I am an Oracle. The Oracle, really. All of them. But that's besides the point. You want to know about Marius.

Marius is one of my best friends. We met years ago, when he tried to kill one of my other best friends as a joke. Thomas thought it was funny; I didn't. I took the poison Marius had used and buried it - most of it. I kept enough for myself, just incase I ever needed to use it on Marius as revenge. I never did. This isn't how most friendships start, I know. But it is how ours started. And if I'm honest, we really became friends the first time that I tried to kill him.

You see, Marius is beloved of Isis, and there are creatures who Her moonlight changes, and - well, I imagine you can guess what he becomes. There are only so many creatures that change with the moon, and turn on friend as if they were foe. He has control, most of the time. Most of the time he fights alongside the rest of the Commission well and as himself. Then sometimes the wolf inside him gets out. It makes him forget everything but the need to fight. But it's okay. I am there with him.

The first time Marius lost control and turned his sword on our friends, I closed my eyes and remembered the time I was King of Scotland, and drew my hammer. I stepped around behind him whilst other people were yelling at him to stop, and I looked for the spot that if I hit it hard enough would kill almost anyone, and I hoped very hard that it wouldn't kill Marius.

It didn't, not that time, and not any of the times after that I had to do it. Once he caught me alone, and I had to draw the sword of a dead man and just watch as hard as I could for where Marius was trying to strike me. I was exhausted after that. But I did beat him in a real fight, and even he admitted it.

I never let him forget that I would be there for him when he needed me. I know what it's like to carry something inside yourself that's so powerful it sometimes overwhelms you. So huge it terrifies you. It is not his fault, and he struggles with it every day.

It is as if we meet, Cateline and I, in the crematorium. She slips between the people around me and takes my hands, and smiles. I know that she can see everything I am feeling as colours that swirl around me. She can see it in everyone. It must be beautiful; a room full of colours, in harmony even though they bear the hues of sadness.

"Blue," she says, because we are one, so she can also hear what I am thinking. "But gold, too, and pink. You are very shiny."

"Thank you." The words come out broken; my throat is too choked with sobs to form them.

The other people around us no longer matter. She steps in and leans her forehead against mine. The lace of her underveil presses against my skin, the silk overveil fluttering against my cheeks. Without them, she is blind, overwhelmed by all of the stories past and present that fill her vision. Originally, this was because the rules of the game said that she couldn't see the future with her veil removed. But for me, it had extra meaning, because I knew what it was like to be so full of thoughts and feelings that you can't break free. To be trapped in looping stories of trauma and hope intertwined.

Now, I am filled with all of my memories of Jack, and all of Cateline's memories of Marius, and the many other people Jack inhabited that she met.

Cateline giggles. "Like the time we looked to the story of the crown of the tall ones and saw him covered in honey."

We laugh. It was one of the more ridiculous visions we were ever given. But - I digress. That isn't the memory she's thinking of. The memory we are thinking of. Heads pressed together, she and I remember the time Marius was dying of the plague, and she offered to kill him.

We are sat on the grass, a good distance from each other, with only our friend Gaivs near us. You see, Marius is sick. Very sick. He's dying of something so contagious that if I so much as reach to hold his hand, I will also die. It all happened very quickly. He and Thomas both caught it, but Thomas was strong enough to fight it off. Thomas is the only one who can go near him now. It's a little ironic.

There is something that can save him. A ritual; but a ritual that you can only take if you're a member of our family. Of the Freemasons. Hemiunu will perform it for him, but first he has to agree to join. Gaivs and I explain it. He will forget if he chooses not to, because of the rites that protect the family, and we explain that too. I beg him to do it. To take this chance at life. To be my brother. My heart feels like it's tearing from my chest because I cannot lose him. I cannot lose him after all the times I have torn the world apart trying to defend him.

He is crying too, when he tells me that he can't, that he won't, that it isn't right. That he would feel more comfort in dying, and that he is not afraid. That he will be with Isis at last, and at peace, with no more of the rage stored up inside him.

I take a deep breath, and promise that if it comes to it, I will kill him myself, quickly and painlessly. I will not let him die a slow and drawn out death to this disease that is taking him from me. My sobs snatch away the edges of the words.

He smiles, and thanks me, and says, "I love you, Cateline."

Jack died later that year. We never played those characters together again, but in the world where the Wasteland Commission exists, Marius lives on as a man who turned his inner rage, the werewolf curse that seemed to damn him, into a righteous fury. Who never backed down from protecting the people that he loved, and from holding true to himself, even as he believed that part of himself was damned. We agreed this - his found family. The people who knew Marius as well as Jack. We didn't want to mourn both; we couldn't contain that much grief. So we comforted ourselves with the knowledge that this man who had been so great a part of Jack still lived on.

Jack and I played other characters together, in the months that remained in his life. But I do not remember them like I remember sitting cross-legged on the grass, promising to kill him quickly. I do not remember them like I remember holding his hands as he listened to some of the last words I ever spoke as Cateline. I do not remember them like I remember my sides hurting from laughing because he and Giles - who was not Giles then, but Gaivs -

were passing around the last of the spicy cheese we'd rotated around the table, everyone taking a bite until it was only the two of them left eating the sticky, saliva-slick lump.

I remember a pink and gold cloth spread out between us, and a deck of cards. Each of them a sheaf of hand-pressed paper, written out painstakingly in dip pen, with dozens of poems from as far back as ancient Sumer. With Jack's hand, Marius picks his past, his present, his future. With my voice, Cateline reads them. It's just like fortune telling; the trick is to get the other person to do all of the talking.

I stand in the crematorium in my partner's arms, Cateline's mind resting upon mine, and listen to what she has to say next. As if she is the only part of me left that can form words.

We are in Avarice's grave and Innovation has told me that he is going to die. To shatter into a hundred thousand pieces and become one with the world, that spark of hope that drives mortalkind to invention and creation. I kneel next to his chair, sob into the side of his leg, and realise then that I will never let him do that alone.

Marius is the one who is there with me. After the vision of my heart fades, Marius holds me as I tremble. I have always known that Innovation is going to die. I have even wondered, since I told the Greatest Story, whether I will live on after this life. My Voice has done its work, now. I am the Last Storyteller. Why would it pass on?

In our hearts, Innovation and I both know that Jerome and Cateline are the last lives we will live.

The tears do not stop until Avarice is dead by my hand and others', until I have fixed one of the worst mistakes Innovation ever made, and set him free of one more burden. It is then that I know what I need to do. It is then that I go to Marius.

His are the ears that I call to listen to the last Fate I will ever write: my own. His are the hands that hold mine as I bind myself to the same destiny as the person I have loved through a hundred lifetimes and more. His is the embrace I step into knowing that one day I, too, will shatter. That the pieces of me will become one with that which they love.

This is the last time Marius will hold me like this. And yet, it also is not. That will not make sense. Let me tell it a different way.

There is a phrase, in roleplaying: suspension of disbelief. It's from Coleridge, originally, and now ubiquitous amongst both roleplayers and those who love the weird or fantastic. He called it "that willing suspension of disbelief for the moment, which constitutes poetic faith".[i] It's a lovely quote. And in roleplaying, it seems on the surface to make sense. Because if I expand those memories, unveil from them the layers of diegesis which shroud that which is not (right now, at least), I will see those things the memory ignores. The electric strip lights that would not be in an ancient Egyptian home. The bright red fire extinguisher. The glowing green sign that reads EXIT.

But there is something else to this, something more that suspension of disbelief does not encompass. I disbelieve in these things that are not part of this shared reality, but only so that I can uphold the belief I have in that reality. I forget the microwave so that I can remember Marius, but I remember Marius because I have chosen to look only at him, at his world, at the world we are building together.

So, when Jack died, we added more bricks to that world he had built with us. Bricks that made sure we would never, ever, forget to believe in it. Bricks that made sure we would never forget to believe in him, a nightingale of belief.

Of course, those bricks are made of our thoughts, our emotions, our memories. Unlike Keats's poetry, this story we have built together is as ephemeral as our lives. I can paint you images and tell you stories of those bricks, but I cannot give you the feeling of building them. I can will Jack to be immortal by believing he is, I can keep his belief going when he is gone - but eventually, I won't be here to believe in him. So will every one of us who upheld that world. And then those bricks, too, will be dust.

[i] Coleridge, S. T. (1817) 'Chapter XIV', in *Biographia Literaria*. Available at: http://www.english.upenn.edu/~mgamer/Etexts/biographia.html (Accessed: 13 November 2020).

These are the things that I think of, standing at his funeral, voice cracking as I try to pour everything I have ever felt and everything Cateline has ever felt into a single song. Body shuddering with sobs. Hands clasping at the people who remain. Mine is the grief of dozens of characters who will never see their friend again; and yet, will always be with them, walking through Egyptian sands, our blades raised to strike down the darkness.

sometimes a lifewalk is not a path you choose;
but one you find yourself on without realising.
sometimes you are partway through a story
before you understand that you are its core.

there is a triangle tower and it is calling us,
home to the islands I knew when they were whole -
when my words were tools and I trod steps
through the veins of the world as it was born anew.

we go because it is in our stories; because we cannot
help but follow the threads of our wakings,
no matter what shadows and whiteness we find
in the land of triangle towers where the first crowns lie.

the Bright Lady shall pass once more, and then
comes the tempest - comes the first of our last steps.
we will stand at the precipice of shadows,
where I cannot shield the nightingale from their colours.

I have not read the stories we will tell beneath our toes.

my hearthfire is yellow, for all that I know of what
has been and what will come is treacle-heavy.
and into these dances go my sisters and my brothers.

and before the brightest tower, the mother's island,
where the largest triangle crown sends us to fly,
we will stand before the echoes of a thousand stories
and we will ask: are we big enough, now?

~ II ~

VOICE AND HEART

How does it start?

Autumn, 1825.

No - that isn't when it starts. It starts in Summer, when Brighton is overflowing with nobles and commoners alike fleeing the acidic rivers of London. There in the capital, a dragon roars, and Theodosia's mothers insist on taking in every fleeing noble the house can stand - plus a few more besides. Anything to gain standing, even in a crisis. Even retired, it's still a show to them.

In London, the dragon falls, and the rain starts.

They pour onto the streets of Brighton when the news comes; Mama drags her out by the hand without a hat or coat or gloves, and Theodosia stumbles, horrified, to the court where the party has already begun in the King's name. Somewhere along the way time blurs - she loses hold of Mama's hand, can no longer see Mother's withering coiffure, and she is left alone in the crowd with a gown so wet it trails mud behind her.

She ends up in the gardens, where the nobles are dancing beneath Canute's rain. It strikes her as odd to celebrate when so many are dead - a defiance that seems to dishonour even as it mourns. The thought, more than the rain, makes her shiver.

Then, the rain stops - for her, at least.

"I appear to have arrived too late to be of much assistance, but I will not have it said that others of the court are to be left without aid."

Theodosia casts her eyes upwards, to the curve of a black umbrella; left, to a weary face partially marked by glittering dragonscale. A flash of courtly recognition - that strange limbo of knowing, but not knowing. She should introduce herself formally, but this doesn't seem like the day for that.

Etiquette is the pillar of a civilised society, her Mother's voice sounds in her head. Theodosia ignores it, and holds out her hand with a different goal in mind.

"I have never been terribly skilled at dancing alone," she lies.

It starts something like that.

I have almost always written in third person when it comes to fiction. I never really thought much about why. It just felt right. At the most, sometimes, I would stray into second person, but for the most part my characters were always a *them* and not an *I*. It took a class of creative writing students asking why I didn't write in first person to make me feel this was abnormal. To force a knot into my chest that was so tight I thought I was going to vomit. I didn't have an answer for them; didn't have a reply to the barrage of *but first person is so much better*.

Almost a year later, I watched a presentation by a woman living with MS. *I*, she said, is too close. Too painful. Too dangerous. *She* is safe. Distant. *She* protects me from *I*. In that moment, I understood why I hate writing in first person.

I also realised why becoming someone else is so deeply transformative, and powerful, and dangerous.

There is a key to understanding how: music.

Music has pulsed through my heart since I was a child. I was raised by musicians, in a house full of music, and could play six instruments by the time I was fifteen. In high school, I arranged a concert version of the film *Moulin Rouge*, extracting the entire band's parts from a piano score. I was certain that I wanted to be a musical director - but then, I was also certain that I wanted to be a writer, an actress, a professor, and several other things.

Then, when I was eighteen, I had a breakdown. The untreated anxiety and depression I had been experiencing for years overflowed, and a year after that, I found myself walking with purpose towards the edge of a station platform. I could feel the rush of the air; the train I hoped would kill me was approaching. Music was not with me then. At least, not the music of my heart. I never stopped listening to it, but bringing out my own music had become intertwined with all the hurts. All of the words that cut into my flesh. All of those steps towards the edge of the train platform.

I found music again because I reached out to it in the third person.

She arrives home late, soaked from head to toe, missing one of the buttons from her collar and still bereft of his name.

"Tesoro mio!" cries Mama, kissing her on both cheeks. "The dragon days are over - is it not wonderful! Come, come, let us get you cleaned up. You are to perform for the Duke tonight!"

Duty claws at Theodosia uncomfortably. "Which Duke?" she asks, not hearing the answer - her mind is still swimming with the spin of the waltz and conversations that go on until dawn and a kiss on the cheek not quite far enough from the lips.

The day becomes a whirl of bathing and dressing and hair and makeup and rehearsal and being squeezed into an exquisite, beaded gown and a carriage too small for the three of them. Her mothers practically glow with delight; another step on the way to the King's favour.

She sings *Parto, parto* to an audience of two hundred - her voice is more dextrous then, it slips over the coloratura without difficulty and earns her a standing ovation from everyone - the Duke included. She brings one hand to her lips, the other to her chest, and dips into a curtsey.

When she stands, her eyes spot light glinting off scales - but it is only a glance. She is swept up by congratulations, her mothers escorting her to meet everyone of note, gushing about how it is only a matter of time before she is invited to perform for the King himself.

The next day, a blue umbrella arrives at the house, tied up by a red ribbon.

The hotel's windows are too small and too stained by years of smoking to let in light. The carpet, which no longer has a distinguishable colour, crunches uncomfortably beneath my too-tight shoes. My first day of work there involves disciplining security guards for watching porn. The manager I am there to assist carries the sharp, stale scent of alcohol with him wherever he goes; I am frequently trapped in a room with his stench. I have multiple panic attacks every day for the one week I manage to work there.

The only place I can be alone is the ladies toilets. The only women in the building are guests, who have their own bathrooms, and the cleaners, who are gone before I arrive. It is a beige room; the seventies happened and it never changed after that. There are too many mirrors that I try not to look at myself in.

At least, I think there are.

This memory might be made up of a dozen different toilets, spaces that I didn't look at because my vision was blurred by tears and I couldn't bear to look up. Still, I can picture it clearly: mustard-yellow sinks on the right, stalls on the left - a barred window at the end, impossible to open, worsening the stench - a combination of stale urine and bleach. Too sharp. Too many mirrors showing my crumpled face and the makeup halfway down my cheeks. I curl away, don't look, stumble against the counter.

I can hear every single sound in the building. This is always the first sign. The first clue that the world is about to disintegrate around me. It steals my breath next; I strain to fill my lungs but nothing happens. That knot in my chest is too tight to let air in. The tears on my cheeks are hot, the snot in my nose is thick, now I can't breathe at all.

I have to breathe, the people who love me would want me to breathe, but all I can think about is how terrible I am, how shameful it is that I'm curled up in the toilets in a hotel that stinks of musty carpets and stale smoke. I was supposed to be more than this. I was supposed to be better. I disconnect. *I* am not longer *I*, *I* has become *she*, *she* is there and broken at my feet.

"Dissociation is a multifaceted concept that describes the separation of normally integrated psychological processes such as emotions, thoughts, memory, or identity.[ii]" It often manifests as a defensive mechanism through which the traumatised person may separate themselves from present or reexperienced pain. In this sense, it is logical and natural; the body and mind are experiencing pain, and dissociation protects the person from that. However, prolonged dissociation can lead to wider anhedonia, or more specific forms of dissociation: dissociative amnesia, dissociative fugue, derealisation, depersonalisation, identity alteration or confusion.

It may be extremely jarring for the individual experiencing it, or it may seem so smooth a transition that the individual does not realise this has happened. Just as you may have found it jarring that I have dropped into an academic voice - or, you might have read on without thinking it strange.

You think we have disconnected from the memory of the panic attack in the toilets. We haven't. These are the thoughts that go through my mind when I separate *I* from *she*.

Now imagine trying to go back to the life of *I* when you are no longer *I*, facing emotions that you cannot connect to but know hurt and hurt and hurt, and you will understand why I kept ending up back in the toilets, hyperventilating, trying to push those feelings back down.

And why, time after time, I always went back to *she*.

Years later, my therapist asks me what I'm feeling when I think about that place.

I am not safe, I say.

Do you ever feel safe? she asks, gently.

I sob *no, no, I never feel safe,* and dissolve into hysterical tears.

I am wrong: I feel safe when I am someone else.

[ii] Pfaltz, M. C. *et al.* (2013) 'Reexperiencing Symptoms, Dissociation, and Avoidance Behaviors in Daily Life of Patients With PTSD and Patients With Panic Disorder With Agoraphobia', *Journal of Traumatic Stress*, 26(4), pp. 443–450.

Two weeks pass, and Theodosia begins to wonder if she dreamt the whole thing.

She whiles away the hours in lessons and rehearsals and performances, not catching so much as a glimpse of him, and it begins to show in her songs. She stops singing Mozart; reaches for Fauré, Saint-Saëns, Flotow, Purcell. If anyone notices, they do not comment on it.

Then one of the Counts hosts a ball - a summer ball, bright colours and joyous music and lights and food and champagne so light it seems to bubble through the head and away with but a drop. Theodosia arrives on the arm of her magic tutor and whiles away two hours dancing and laughing and joking with her - until someone asks the older mage for a dance, and Theodosia is left in her own kind of silence.

"I have never liked dancing alone," murmurs a voice, and her heart leaps.

She looks up, wonders if she should have worn a different dress; one that flows with movement. She wants to fly. "I didn't bring my umbrella," she says, and takes his hand.

"Well," he says, striding past her and leading her into the centre of the ballroom, "at least you have one to forget."

They dance; his hand holds her a little more tightly around the waist than it should. He lowers his lips a little closer to her ear to speak than he needs to, even here at the heart of the ballroom. Their steps are quick, precise, but Theodosia barely focuses on them at all - all she can think about is the heat of his body, and wonder if it comes from the dragonscale on his face, or something else. Like her.

When he spins her out to the side of the room, his lips part as if to speak; another voice interrupts them.

"Dosia, piccola! You look so beautiful when dancing the polka. But who is your fine partner?"

Her throat tightens. Mother will expect her to introduce him, but she cannot. How can she explain that? They should have introduced themselves to one another the moment they met. It was raining; that hardly seems an excuse now.

"Francis Leveson-Gower," he pronounces, letting go of Theodosia's hand to reach for Mother's and then Mama's, kissing them with perfect courtly poise.

She tries to ignore the way the bottom has dropped out her stomach. "Your lordship," she states, gesturing to the women across from her, "my mother, Alessandra Bordoni, and my mother, Maria Bianchini."

"Ah, I thought I recognised your face. I believe you performed for my family some years ago, Ms. Bianchini."

The two of them glow with pride that their powder and poise fails to conceal. A thousand thoughts flood through Theodosia's mind, the word *nobleman* the damned refrain in them all. This is trouble. He is trouble. She should smile politely and say that it was a chance meeting and never see him again. But her lips have his name now and her heart is soaring and oh, oh no.

"In fact," Theodosia says, lifting her head and smiling at Francis, all politeness and not a hint of anything more, "we were just discussing the possibility of a performance. His lordship was at the Duke's soirée, and is quite fond of Mozart."

They discuss little of substance for a time until the two older women swan away - soon enough to leave the guests wanting more, late enough not to be rude. Theodosia feels the breath escape her chest, and the knot in her throat crash to her chest.

"I don't recall discussing a performance," Francis remarks, head tilted as he looks after her mothers. "Why did you lie?"

She looks away. There's no purpose in trying to respond to a question you don't have all of an answer for. He steps around in front of her, making a show of allowing a nearby dancing couple past. The woman's dress ripples over Theodosia's own and startles her from her silence.

"It felt like I ought to."

He looks at her so intently that she notices even with her eyes cast down. "Traditionally, one lies when one has something to hide."

"I will concede that point," she says, eyes flicking up. It feels like she's burning. "I suppose that would make my lie a lie - after all, we hardly have anything to hide."

Francis stares at her for a moment longer, then looks out into the ballroom. He opens his mouth - to agree, she thinks, to make his excuses and leave. Instead, he says, "Would you like to?"

That. That's how it starts.

Years after I don't step in front of a train, and years before I realise that I have never felt safe, I put on a different suit of armour and step into the upstairs room of a small pub in central London. The armour is not just literal armour, but another character: Morgana, sister to Merlin and the Dragon - an immortal being who was slain by her brother when a ritual went wrong, and returned only centuries later.

When I am weaving Morgana into being, I take threads of the music in my heart and intertwine them with her ambition and drive and lies upon lies. I am brave enough, now, to open up that part of my heart again - but only if *I* lie, too. Only if it looks like her heart, not mine. I walk into the first session holding a ukulele case, and spend month upon month singing acoustic covers, whilst the rest of the characters discuss political machinations and dramatic backstories.

It makes my heart soar. I can feel that love coming back

to me, the love I thought had been taken away by years of trauma. I start singing outside of the game, too - on late-night Skype calls to friends, to my family, at house parties. It feels like homecoming. My heart is made of music again.

When I go to my next game session, I open my mouth to sing Mozart. This is a true demonstration of my courage: I grew up singing classical in choirs, and had always feared I wasn't skilled enough, that I wasn't as good as the people who had actually taken singing lessons. Finally, I have the chance to do it again, in a place where I am confident and comfortable, somewhere where I can -

"If you're going to do that," someone says loudly, "you could at least do it in tune."

I stop singing.

Not just then, as I fight not to have a panic attack in front of everyone, tear off my armour both literal and figurative and all but run home.

Not just at that game, though I do never go back there, the character now sullied by the comment. It was meant in-character. That doesn't matter. The words have punched through the frames of reality and hit me in the heart. I have opened the link between Morgana and I with music, and the words attack me in that weak point.

She has become too close to *I* and now the world has

used *she* to hurt me. I am not safe. Even when I am someone else. I cannot escape it.

I stop singing on Skype calls, to friends, to family, at house parties.

I stop singing at all.

Summer becomes Autumn and it becomes easier to lie. Theodosia and Francis learn the patterns of the people around them and develop their own - her mothers are away on Tuesdays at their club, the servants in his house leave for the day at eleven, if you turn down the right street on the way to the court you will find the spot where the lamps are never quite fully lit.

Opportunity sends them both into the Connected Realms and, somehow, he manages to find a lake. She lights up so much at the sight of it that for a moment he can hear the sound of waves crashing against rocks, as if just being near the water again had made something in her heart call towards it.

They stay by the water into the night. She tells him her true name, the name of her heart - Aglaopheme, siren of the lambent voice, of lost rocks and ever-present shackles. He presses his lips to the pearls and silver in her hair; the stones are cold.

In the morning, they walk around the lake again as if they had simply strolled there after breakfast, then return to Brighton. He sends her a bouquet of pale roses filled with glittering pearls on wire stems, and she tells her mothers that the gift is a thank you for her latest performance.

September becomes October and a letter arrives, inviting her to perform for the King. She opens it over breakfast and, a few moments later, brings up toast and bile. Her mothers attribute it to overwhelming delight.

Theodosia knows better.

When I was in the darkest parts of my mental and emotional healing, my brother gave me a piece of marble. It was the sort of thing designed to sit on a desk, or serve as a paperweight. The text on it read: *never, never, never give up*. Years later, when he was struggling for sobriety, I gave him it back, so that he could remember it too.

One of the things that is hardest to reconcile when experiencing mental illness is the concept of giving up. Because it can feel like you are giving up constantly; every time you crawl back into bed, or miss another appointment, or blurt out another intrusive thought you didn't really want to verbalise.

But giving up is not the same as failing, and failing does not make you a failure. The trouble with mental illness, especially those made of depression, is that you stop seeing the world in colour. There is only white - absolute, perfect success - and black - catastrophic, all-encompassing failure. There is no in-between. There is only this. Good and bad. Black and white. Worthiness and worthlessness. If you fail, nothing you ever succeeded at matters anymore.

The world is made of these binaries, and all of them are terrible - because all of them are overlaid upon this notion that one side is heavier than the other. One side is worthier than the other. One side is *better* than the other. And those in the smaller side - women, disabled, people of colour - are inferior, whilst those in-between are nothing at all. The darkness is not one side of that binary. The darkness is the existence of the binary itself.

Turning to face that darkness and laying down in it: that is what giving up looks like. Not falling into it in the first place.

When you relearn to see the world in colour, or at least in shades of grey, you start to see the difference. You see that the times where everything was too much, and you went freefall into the pit of worthlessness again, are not the same as giving up. They are stumbling blocks. And what makes you strong is not what you endure within there. It is not the pain. We are not transformed into better people by the pain. Pain is not a force to be used for personal growth, and we are worth more - made of more - than the pain we have endured.

We are strong because we get back out of the pit. Because we do not give up. No matter how long it takes.

Sometimes, my larp characters heal me entirely by accident. Cateline takes me by surprise - a gift I had not expected to receive, a twin I had not expected to create.

When I write Theodosia into being, I do everything deliberately.

The hurt in my heart, the wound upon that singing voice I packed away, has turned to anger. Anger that I worked so hard to recover something so precious, and someone destroyed it in a moment. Rage that the place where I felt safe, the *way* that I felt safe there, became a way to hurt me. Fury that all of these years that I could have been singing were now silenced.

I take all of that rage and fury and bind it up into a woman. A woman who comes from a line of enslaved sirens, their voices held captive by masters who used them to sink the ships of their enemies. A woman who dared to love someone she should not, and in the face of putting him at risk, accepted her own destruction instead. A woman who gave up everything to protect the daughter he gave her, including her voice.

And one day, stepped out into a deadly Wasteland, hoping to find that voice again.

Whilst as Cateline I had spoken only in metaphor, as Theodosia I cast magic spells only by singing. In larp, spellcasting is often represented by verbal invocations. These might be standardised, or made up by the caster at the time. In the game where I create Theodosia, there is nothing saying I cannot sing my spells. So I do.

It's dark when the game begins, and I am in a ballgown that has already soaked up to the knee because of how heavily it's raining. I have her umbrella shaking in my hand, and dozens of blue and green threads bound to my person - representing bound forces of water and air, which I will then use to power my spells. As we move, our company packs into a single group to keep the more fragile safe - and then, we come under attack.

This is it. This is the moment where I decide if I can do this or not.

Only I don't have to decide at all. I have already made Theodosia. I have already become Theodosia. And Theodosia is one of the finest opera singers in London, and she is not going to be enslaved like her great great grandmothers had been, her voice given to someone else to control - to silence.

So Theodosia and I open my mouth, and my heart, and we sing.

There are flowers waiting in the dressing room of the theatre before her next performance. Roses again - white this time, devoid of pearls. She opens the card underneath them and pushes down the returning urge to vomit, in favour of sending lightning crackling from her fingers.

Miss Bordoni,

It is with regret that I write to convey the following on behalf of my son and family; an act which I undertake with no small displeasure, for amongst the Court your own family are held in high regard. Nonetheless, in light of the information that has come to my attention, I cannot forego this duty.

My son is a good man - an excellent man, of noble bearing and worthy of the lineage of which he is a part. He is destined for great things, and his ambitions credit that quality with their high reach. I have no doubt that, years from now, we shall commend him for his appointment to Parliament as is his most fervent desire.

Such a man, as Francis shall surely become, will bear the burden of expectation. Heir or not, Francis is a product of a noble line that stretches back generations. He bears the mark and blood of that most noble and English of creatures, the White Dragon.

For his honour, for his reputation, and for his duty to that lineage, Francis must marry, and he must marry well. You will understand, I am sure, that some people are simply born higher than others. Only the uncouth seek to tear them down.

I hope, Miss Bordoni, that you are not such a person. The common born provide great service to the King in his Court, and yet they are ever but one thing: their reputation. A fine reputation rests against your name, and your mothers', to your great credit.

Which comes to the crux of the matter. That which I have heard, Miss Bordoni, portrays you as little more than a common whore. One who has corrupted my noble son with such foul influence as to make him little more than a strung puppet. I have faithful reports from those who, having travelled to the Queen's Park this past week, have reports of witnessing such lewd acts that I cannot bring myself to name them.

However, I am not cruel. It would bring me no pleasure to destroy you, though it is within my power to do so. I will instead trust that your love for my son is great enough that you shall value his future, if not your own, and do what is right. Were there to be no future association between the two of you, I should be quite satisfied.

I hope, madam, that you shall weigh the consequences of these sins heavily upon your soul, for the Gods alone shall judge you for them.

George Leverson-Gower
1st Lord of Sutherland

The words burn like his touch, a heat that had always seemed so different to her raging storm, beautiful in its disjointed reflection - now marred by the searing fire of his father's words, which paint the image of everything she has ever feared she might be.

It takes four attempts for her to fold the card back down; to tuck it somewhere it will not be found. To take the roses that she knows mean grace and humility and other things she doesn't feel right now, and hurl them wholesale into the fireplace.

She sings Handel to a crowd of four hundred, her voice so full of emotion that she cracks all of the high notes, and hates both the secrets in her hands and the one growing inside her.

The next day, in-between retching into the chamber-pot, she makes a plan. She needs a better lie. A lie so good that even Francis will believe it. Because he is a good man, and good men are destroyed by the truth, and she will do anything to stop him from enduring it. His father is right; she does love him that much. She has to. She has no choice.

The nausea passes. She puts on the sort of dress that would earn Mama's approval and Mother's horror, takes a carriage across the realm, and weeps her way into the bed of a handsome courtier of little consequence and worse reputation - who disappoints her three times before she escapes at dawn.

Within two days the gossips in the court have done all the work for her. Scandal flies out from her like a backdraft of flame. The invitation from the King is quietly retracted; she stops leaving the house. She stops singing. She stops doing much of anything at all, but for waiting. No more flowers arrive. No more cards. No more umbrellas. There is only the silence, and the truth, veiled by a thousand lies.

A month later she goes sobbing into Mama's arms, hands clutched against her growing abdomen. The lie is complete.

And that...that is how it ends.

There is a concept in roleplaying called bleed. It is not specific to larping, but it is of greater significance to larp due to the increased immersion that the physical aspect of larping adds. There is something powerful about reaching out to touch someone's arm, rather than just saying, "my character reaches out to touch your character's arm". That viscerality is part of what makes up bleed.

"Bleed comes in two major forms: bleed-in – when the emotions, thoughts, relationship dynamics, and physical states of the player affect the character – and bleed-out, the opposite process.[iii]" Bleed occurs almost constantly, and to absolutely everyone - no matter what kind of roleplayer they are, or what kind of character they are playing.

"Bleed," she writes, "is neither inherently negative nor positive." Bleed can be everything from feeling anger at a player because their character betrayed yours, to experiencing romantic feelings towards a player because your characters are in a romantic relationship. And these will be the most basic, most frequently cited examples you'll find of bleed. Both are potentially negative - depending on your circumstances, and the other player's, and your ability to navigate those feelings.

I have experienced negative bleed, too. You can consider the moment someone told me not to sing off key to be an example of negative bleed. I have had both of the feelings I just mentioned, and a million more besides. I have had games where my mental illness has bled into my performance of my character - my ability to empathise as a character affected by anhedonia, or my motivation as a character sapped by my lack of it.

We talk about negative bleed, in larp. Many games have a debrief built into them, where players can exorcise the feelings their characters brought up for them. When Theodosia and Francis have a shouting match across a room, his player and I find a moment to check on each other. When we find ourselves made anxious by the other's absence even a few days after the game has ended, we are honest about it, because we know that bleed can be bad and must be taken seriously.

But roleplayers so rarely talk about the good bleed.

The first time I ever sang a full song as Theodosia, not just a scrap of spellcasting but a full aria, I was shaking from head to toe. It was incredibly cold, and we were all drenched from the rain, and I was wearing a foolishly flimsy ballgown - to many people, I imagine it looked like I was just shivering. It wasn't a huge problem - Theodosia was nervous too. But she and I stood tall, and remembered that we were more than our fears, and we sang.

It wasn't perfect. We were singing Dido's lament, from Purcell's *Dido and Aeneas*. I have been singing all of my life, but I have no classical training, save for a couple of decades of being in choirs. It was so cold that our voice was a little thin and reedy, but the cold made the vibrato in it even stronger.

Thy hand, Belinda! Darkness shades me. On thy bosom, let me rest.

When I was scared, Theodosia was scared with me. As the years went on, we began to sing songs that were harder and harder. We sang an eight minute aria from Berlioz's *La damnation de Faust*. We sang *Après un Rêve* to Francis, filling the words with all of Theodosia's passion and fury, before storming away in tears and trembling that was both hers and mine. I fled across the field of the scout camp and into the toilets; there, I exhaled Theodosia's sorrow and my anxiety. The anxiety faded only because her sorrow had, too - her sadness swelling as my fears dimmed.

We sang, and we sang, and Theodosia's voice bled mine back into being.

[iii] Bowman, S. L. (2015) *Bleed: The spillover between player and character.* Available at: https://nordiclarp.org/2015/03/02/bleed-the-spillover-between-player-and-character/ (Accessed: 13 November 2020).

~ III ~

SHIELD ON ARM

The pain stops immediately.

She's cornered him, the shimmering walls of his realm now his prison. He won't get past her. He won't escape. And most of all, he won't take another soul from her world.

Penny has always known she has the capacity to absorb more power than she can contain. It's just the same as pushing yourself past the point of exhaustion. And power is power is power. It doesn't need to be a spell, not really. Believe something hard enough, and you can make anything reality.

Well. At least, *she* can.

So as the Demon Lord's power yanks souls from the victims of her friends, Penny extends her own power and grabs them. Holds them. Shelters them. It doesn't matter who they were in life - cultists, murderers. Life is sacred, no matter whose life it is. She remembers that. She still believes it. She never stopped.

Soon there are dozens of souls contained within her, and it should hurt - it should be agonising. Her body has torn itself away from her own soul, her own power, there isn't even any blood left within it - her blood is part of her soul now, its ancient strength all that is holding the others close to her.

It is alright now, Peronel, her God says in the immortal threads of her heart, and Penny smiles. He is the reason it does not hurt. He is the reason she is strong enough to shelter them. She is nothing but light.

It's easier to fight when you're not worrying about trying to parry blows. The Demon Lord's sword slices through her flesh and Penny barely flinches. Instead she lunges forward, her blade an extension of her arm, remembering all of the advice her father ever gave her even as she forgets it. *Don't let your guard down, child,* his memory whispers in her ear. Penny grins, an incongruous and ridiculous expression, and lets the Demon Lord take every opening. Every chance.

None of the blows sway her. All of his spells, his power, simply get absorbed into her form. All of the souls he calls to him, that he desperately tries to grab, step instead into the embrace of her God.

The next strike is the one that kills her. It doesn't hurt, but she feels something all the same, from the dozens of people whose souls touch her own - sighs and gasps and sadness and something unfamiliar; pride.

As dead as a mercenary can be, with all of her vitae drained from her at last, Penny keeps fighting.

Roleplaying as a hobby has always been surrounded by fear. Imaginative play is not inherently damned - it is used in classrooms for both young and old as a way to teach all manner of skills. But when you transform it into a game, something seems to change.

There are extremes, of course. And whilst I don't want to judge something just by its extremes - to just compare Dungeons and Dragons as the progenitor of all roleplaying with the moral panic that condemned it as a Satanistic practice - it is hard to break free of that legacy.

But even more than that, the thing about roleplaying is that its detractors are contradictory. Roleplayers are condemned for roleplaying things that should not exist, like murder and other lesser crimes, or religious practices both lifted from the world and fictional. They are told that they could get 'stuck' in their characters, forget who they are, abandon all responsibilities.

And yet, at the same time, they are told that their fictional worlds are not real. That there is real life and there are their games.

This forgets the most important thing: all roleplaying is real life. If I run up to you, dressed as a peasant, and beg you for help because the neighbouring kingdom have sent troops over the border - I really have run up to you and said that. The fact that we are both pretending to be other people does not change the fact that we are both there, physically, pretending.

Meeting your friends every week for a game of Dungeons and Dragons is real. The stories you create are real because they exist as something you have made together. They are also fictional. Just because something is fictional does not mean it is not real.

Here is the thing that I think is dangerous: if you tell people that their fictional worlds are not real, and tell them also that they must not get lost within those fictional worlds, that they must remember their responsibilities to the real world, then they will forget some important things.

Because the vast majority of games, the ones that we're really talking about, involve other people. And any time you involve other people, you involve a degree of responsibility. I have run live-action games with almost a hundred people. A team of five to write and run the game; a team of twenty-five or so to act out the creatures that the players will encounter; up to fifty people to be those players. And this is far from the size that live-action games to get to. There are events held in Europe for thousands of people, where entire towns are built in fields.

Every single one of those people is there to enter a fictional world, but they have a responsibility to all of the others around them. To turn up on time. To adhere to the rules of the game. To respect others in what they choose to roleplay.

The moment you start telling people this is not real life is the very moment that they will forget those responsibilities. It is the very moment that they will call someone a slur and say 'oh, it's just what my character would do'. It is the moment that they will get angry and that weapon blow lands hard enough to injure. It is the moment that they will turn up to their high fantasy game wearing Converse trainers because who cares, it's only your shoes. It is the moment that they will forget issues of accessibility, a problem that plagues the live-action world, because 'the medieval world wasn't accessible'.

All that you have done is made the person into the very thing you claimed they were. But they did not have to be. It is possible to immerse yourself into a character whilst never forgetting that you are still yourself, that the people around you are still themselves, even though they are dressed as goblins and coming at you with knives - in the same way you do not forget those knives are not metal, but latex over foam over carbon fibre.

Penny was one of the first characters I ever started, in the first game I ever went to. Over the years, she changed as much as I did. She went from being a pacifist priestess, to rediscovering her skills as a psychic assassin - awakening in a manner not unlike a sleeper agent. From light and love and peace, she stepped into shades of grey - to moral ambiguity and uncertainty. In time, she became one of the leaders of the Inquisition, a group that investigate supernatural power in her world and ensured it is contained.

She became a Magiarch - an exceptionally powerful ritualist. Her speciality was that she was capable of absorbing any kind of supernatural power into her own body for her own use. With this skill she could defend others, taking spells meant to harm them; she could transform one kind of power into another, solving any problem; she was a polymath of the supernatural, reading and using all the power that her world had to offer.

And all through this, she struggled with the core of herself. Born into a noble family, in a world where nobility entailed a special kind of power in one's blood, Penny was a traditionalist. She had ambition not only in her career, but in the rest of her life. She wanted to get married, to have children, and to finally get the life she had thought was lost when her family died. She fell in love regularly, and often, and with people who had no interest in her whatsoever - or who weren't acceptable candidates for marriage. After all, she was a noble - she was meant to marry someone like her.

She didn't. She fell in love with an angel, a man who seemed to find it easy to be all of the things she struggled with - goodness and kindness and strength and courage. No matter what happened, he continued to fight on, fearless and determined.

Loving him made Penny happy. It gave her balance, where her ambition made her strive to give everything to everyone and save nothing for herself. But most of all, loving him taught her that she had always been brave. She had always been strong. She had always been good.

No two larps are the same.

This is not only by design; it is by the very nature of larping. Larps are a collaboratively created experience. "Role-play is ephemeral", write Stenros and Montola.[iv] They explain that larp is not inherently an artifact, though there may be artifacts of larp - such as the rule books or setting books on which they are based. It is an experience. It is "impossible to truly document", they add, because it is an embodied experience. This has made it difficult to study larps academically. In producing a long-term project on volunteering for a larp organisation, Mitchell writes that her "fieldnotes were therefore frequently produced immediately upon leading the setting".[v] It was impossible to record her thoughts in real time, and even her experience is but one angle on something multifaceted.

This inherently non-linear nature makes even two larps that are otherwise identical - in setting, participants, and all other aspects prepared in advance - completely dissimilar to one another. It is impossible that every single participant will make the same decisions at every moment; that the environment will behave in the same precise way. And, of course, you do not often get larps that are identical in all ways but their embodied existence. The difference between UK larp, US larp, EU larp and more are so vast that anyone travelling from one to the other would suffer from the lack of understanding. No game provides every bit of data necessary to participate - there will always be an extent to which it inherits the assumptions of that gaming culture.

This is seen especially in Nordic larp. Viewed by many outside its circles in a mixture of reverence and disbelief, Nordic larp is characterised by its unique approach. Nordic larp is where you find the strange experiments. It is where you find the games that look at the frames of roleplay and, rather than working out how to play within them, wonder how they can break them.

In 2008, Tobias Wrigstad created a larp game called - and about - *Gang rape*. Montola describes it as "an intentionally repulsive short scenario that examines gang rape as a particularly ugly form of violence".[vi] It has three scenes: the lead up to the rape, the rape itself, and the aftermath. Though it does not contain a literal rape, the entire game is set up to create an intense embodied experience, and the rules actively enable this.

This probably sounds strange, and awful. Why on earth

would anyone want to play out a rape, even through narration? Why would you choose to experience a rape victim's emotions, or a rapist's?

In the early 1930s, a French dramatist by the name of Antonin Artaud published his manifesto for *Le théâtre de la cruauté* - the Theatre of Cruelty. Simultaneously a wide-reaching denouncement of theatre, and a celebration of his belief in its immense power, it was received with a great deal of confusion. His letters, published later in *Le Théâtre et son Double*[vii] show his critics querying everything from the definition of cruelty to the supposed gratuity of his violent manifesto.

There is no doubt, reading Artaud's work, that he was a stark pessimist. In one of his letters, whilst defending his definition of cruelty, he stated that "Effort is a cruelty, existence through effort is a cruelty." Later, he described evil as a permanent cosmic law, and good only as "one more cruelty added to the other." It is this omnipresence of evil that Artaud wished the theatre to face.

It was not out of sadism. He believed that if the theatre did not reflect that cruelty then it was not serving its purpose: as a bridge between dream and reality. Through theatre, he wished to perform something of an exorcism. To expose humanity to its true nature, and doing so create "a living whirlwind that devours the darkness". In a way, *Gang rape* can be viewed through this lens. Montola describes it as "a demonstration of the fact that 'we all have the capacity to fantasize about these things'".

It should be noted, of course, that this is a generous interpretation of Theatre of Cruelty. Artaud's manifesto demands the casting off of so many hallmarks of theatre that it is no wonder his critics thought it ridiculous – which may very well apply to Wrigstad's game, too.

And when you understand how much larp can vary, and how some of it dances on a knife's edge, you understand how easy it can be to get it wrong.

[iv] Stenros, J. and Montola, M. (2011) 'The making of Nordic Larp: Documenting a tradition of ephemeral co-creative play', in. *Proceedings of DiGRA 2011 Conference: Think Design Play*, Utrecht School of the Arts, The Netherlands.

[v] Mitchell, L. (2019) 'Volunteers as monstrous workers: "monsters" in UK live-action roleplay game organizations.', *Culture & Organisation*, 25(3), pp. 233–248.

[vi] Montola, M. (2010) 'The positive negative experience in extreme role-playing', in. *Nordic DiGRA 2010 Conference*, Stockholm, Sweden. Available at: http://www.digra.org/wp-content/uploads/digital-library/10343.56524.pdf (Accessed: 13 November 2020).

[vii] Artaud, A. (1958) *The Theatre and its Double*. New York, NY: Grove Press, Inc.,

The angel that Penny loved taught her she was already brave - and, in turn, Penny taught me that I was, too.

She joined an order called the Knights of the Land, a group devoted to protecting people who could not protect themselves. There she met more people who were good, and strong, and brave. The order was known for its fearlessness, for its determination, and for its oath: *Shield on arm, sword in hand, brothers together, we defend the land.* They were her family.

The more I played Penny, and the more I played Penny with other Knights, the more I embraced my own bravery. I saw that I was just as protective of the people I loved, just as determined, just as able to keep fighting even when it felt like everything was lost. The Knights extended beyond the game, and so did its family.

Month by month by year, when Penny would put herself at risk to save others, I realised this part of her came from me. Even when it went wrong. Even when Penny's crushes went so badly that I felt hurt by the rejection. Even when I felt like the character was getting too complex, too Mary Sue. Even when I felt like Penny was just *too much*, I still had that growing belief in my own courage. Even when I couldn't get out of bed except to go to larp games, or roleplay with my friends online, Penny reminded me that I was still worthy. That my life was worth something.

Without Penny, I do not think I would be alive.

At Jack's funeral, months after Penny had died, we shouted the Knights' oath into the rafters of the crematorium, voices broken with grief.

Now, whenever I need to be brave, I ask Jack to help me - but most of the time, it's Penny who answers.

I have often found that I want different things from roleplay. There is an old theory called the threefold model, later revised as the three way model.[viii] This model, revised by Petter Bøckman, posits that there are three approaches to roleplaying. Dramatists, who value the storyline; Gamists, who value solving plot and challenges; Immersionists, who value the role's life. Nobody will be solely in one camp. In all likelihood, they will have tendencies to all three, with different weightings. For example, I am primarily a Dramatist, but use some Immersionist concepts in my approach to that storytelling - and whilst I am not there 'to win', so not fully a Gamist, it is still important to me that my characters' abilities reflect their composition in story and immersion.

Bøckman identifies one of the challenges as this: "it is when the preferred state of play by the players collide with that of organisers, or that of other players, that things may go wrong". Which is to say when I, a Dramatist/Immersionist, enter a game run primarily by Gamist players, I feel that disconnect. That was my experience of a lot of roleplay games for a long time. Eventually I found people who were closer to my school of thought, but the friends I had already made still did not share it.

Sometimes, I didn't realise this. Because no one is entirely absent from all three categories – so I would see glimpses of a person's desire to create a wonderful, dramatic story with me, and miss that it was not all that they wanted.

Writing is how I express myself, and I cannot play a character unless I have written them. For Penny, I wrote for years - tens of thousands of words - a hundred thousand, all for someone who had shown an interest in her and her story. Someone who had let me into that small, brief glimpse.

I wrote so much, and so loudly, that I never stopped to listen for his silence. For the moment that he stopped saying much in reply. The moment that he stopped saying much to me at all.

One day, he said to me: I'm sorry. I just don't feel comfortable playing them right now.

I'm still not sure if he ever did.

And now, every time I think of Penny, it hurts.

[viii] Bøckman, P. (2003) 'The Three-Way Model: Revision of the Threefold Model', in *As larp grows up—Theory and methods in larp*. Copenhagen: BookPartner.

She can see the end coming; her body is ruined now, with nothing left to mend its wounds. A stiff breeze and she'll be nothing but a beacon of light. But there is one more thing she has to do. One more person she has to protect. She left a shell of herself with her friends, not able to leave them even when she's decided to.

The shell stands, blade in her hand, staring down the best friend of the angel she has loved since the day she met him. Tidas has been marked by the Demon Lord - if she doesn't keep him angry enough, then the moment the Demon Lord dies, he will die too. His face is rage, but his eyes are bright with gratitude.

"I won't let you get to them," she says, as their God takes over Tidas's soul. "You won't hurt them, I promise."

Tidas crashes into the shell like a tidal wave, but she holds herself strong - forces all that she has left of her might into keeping its body steady. The lights of her ritual room wink out in Sellaville; it's costing all of her power to do it. Every ritual she's ever cast, every empowerment, she pulls all of them to her to keep it going.

Around them, their friends stand back, letting Penny be the shield at last. Letting her protect one friend from another.

It takes so long - she can hear a fight behind her body. But then there's a cry of "Now!" and her sword is striking true - not the one in her hands where she stands fighting her brother, but the one she thrusts into the heart of the Demon Lord.

It isn't her that kills him, truly. It's Purity. The part of Imrazil, their God, that has always understood her more than any other of His Virtues. The one who has always looked at her and said: keep trying. It is impossible, but keep trying.

The world turns blue. Or at least, she imagines it does; a shower of rose petals that covers the destruction of the plane around her soul.

She opens her eyes; looks into Tidas's face. "It's alright," she says, as Imrazil fades from him, too. On a dying plane, she lets the sheltered souls go. Now they are all safe. Now, at last, she has done enough. "You're okay."

Death consumes her before she can feel her knees buckle.

As she ceases to exist, Penny stumbles onto a crossroads of light. To her left, she can see her family - her birth family, all of them, smiling and waving, preserved as they were the day they died. She could go to them. She could be with them again, at last.

Instead she steps forward. She steps towards Imrazil. Towards the God who has lived in every inch of the Oath she took and never regretted. God of Virtue; God of shields and siblings and friends. Behind Him, she can see every Knight she's ever known; just silhouettes against infinite light. All of the people who have stood by her no matter what she has been, no matter what she has done. All of the people who showed her she was brave, even when she thought she wasn't.

They are worth it. They are worth everything.

Imrazil offers her His hand.

Penny takes it.

REFERENCES

[i] Coleridge, S. T. (1817) 'Chapter XIV', in *Biographia Literaria*. Available at: http://www.english.upenn.edu/~mgamer/Etexts/biographia.html (Accessed: 13 November 2020).

[ii] Pfaltz, M. C. *et al.* (2013) 'Reexperiencing Symptoms, Dissociation, and Avoidance Behaviors in Daily Life of Patients With PTSD and Patients With Panic Disorder With Agoraphobia', *Journal of Traumatic Stress*, 26(4), pp. 443–450.

[iii] Bowman, S. L. (2015) *Bleed: The spillover between player and character*. Available at: https://nordiclarp.org/2015/03/02/bleed-the-spillover-between-player-and-character/ (Accessed: 13 November 2020).

[iv] Stenros, J. and Montola, M. (2011) 'The making of Nordic Larp: Documenting a tradition of ephemeral co-creative play', in. *Proceedings of DiGRA 2011 Conference: Think Design Play*, Utrecht School of the Arts, The Netherlands.

[v] Mitchell, L. (2019) 'Volunteers as monstrous workers: "monsters" in UK live-action roleplay game organizations.', *Culture & Organisation*, 25(3), pp. 233–248.

[vi] Montola, M. (2010) 'The positive negative experience in extreme role-playing', in. *Nordic DiGRA 2010 Conference*, Stockholm, Sweden. Available at: http://www.digra.org/wp-content/uploads/digital-library/10343.56524.pdf (Accessed: 13 November 2020).

[vii] Artaud, A. (1958) *The Theatre and its Double*. New York, NY: Grove Press, Inc.,

[viii] Bøckman, P. (2003) 'The Three-Way Model: Revision of the Threefold Model', in *As larp grows up—Theory and methods in larp*. Copenhagen: BookPartner.

ACKNOWLEDGEMENTS & NOTES

This work was completed as a dissertation for my MA in Creative Writing with the University of Kent at Canterbury. As such, I am indebted most of all to my incredible supervisor, Dorothy Lehane. Without Dorothy's support and guidance this work would not be what it is, especially given the great challenges and traumas that were faced during its production. For similar reasons, I am grateful also to the wonderful School of English and the Creative Writing team at Kent for their support, as well as my mentor, Helen.

Thank you to Labyrinthe, Frail Realities, and the various individuals and groups who have run larp events for or with me in the past decade and a half of being a goblin. Special thanks must go also to those whose characters appear in this work - some of whom are named within it, and some of whom are not. I trust that you will have recognised yourselves (or your other selves, as it were) and smiled accordingly.

For holding me together in the worst year of my life, I am grateful beyond words to my husband Tiffer, who is an infinite source of love and support in a very thorny world. To my best friend and twin Jo, who believes in me when I cannot believe in myself. To our beautiful compassion coven: Jo, Wei, Beck and Steph, for giving me somewhere to scream and cry. To my family, both sides thereof, for loving me no matter what.

If any of the trauma or distress that I have related in this book has resonated with you, I hope that you are receiving the love and care you need. If you are not, please consider seeking it out. You can easily search for mental health support online and find local services or therapists to help you through the never-ending journey that is healing. The journey is long and hard, and sometimes it goes down as well as up, but you can do it. Remember that sometimes, the things that help most are those you don't expect.

Oh, and one last thing: please don't try eating raw lavender, even if a dragon dares you to.

Rebecca Milton is an author from south-east England who grew up hiding in a myriad of fantastical worlds.

When she was studying for her Batchelor's Degree, she discovered tabletop roleplaying through a university society, beginning her roleplaying career as a halfling thief called Jemima. She soon progressed to larping (or LARPing, or LRPing, as you prefer), eventually finding a home within the cavie family of the Labyrinthe Live Roleplaying club in Chislehurst, and the wonderful crew of Pilgrims at Frail Realities. Given that these clubs led her to meet her eventual husband, she's pretty sure she owes them her life at this point.

She now lives in Kent with her husband and their cat, Princess-General Leia, and is currently studying for a PhD in the Medical Humanities with the University of Kent at Canterbury.

www.ingramcontent.com/pod-product-compliance
Lightning Source LLC
Chambersburg PA
CBHW071506070526
44578CB00001B/454